Good Work for Small Hands

poems by

Michelle Delaine Williams

Finishing Line Press
Georgetown, Kentucky

Good Work
for Small Hands

Copyright © 2023 by Michelle Delaine Williams
ISBN 979-8-88838-152-6 First Edition
All rights reserved under International and Pan-American Copyright Conventions. No part of this book may be reproduced in any manner whatsoever without written permission from the publisher, except in the case of brief quotations embodied in critical articles and reviews.

ACKNOWLEDGMENTS

Many thanks to the editors of the following publications in which these poems first appeared:

"Gale Force Winds" and "What's in a Shed?," *RAIN Magazine*, 2019
"Hunger," *Verseweavers*, 2016

Special thanks to Quinton Hallet for awarding "Hunger" first place in the New Poets category of the 2016 Oregon Poetry Association's fall contest.

Also deep gratitude to all my mentors at the Attic Institute of Arts and Letters and the Ambassador Poetry Seminars. And, of course, to my beloved first reader, Curtis Settino.

Publisher: Leah Huete de Maines
Editor: Christen Kincaid
Cover Art: © Can Stock Photo/cloud rain
Author Photo: Curtis C. Settino
Cover Design: Elizabeth Maines McCleavy

Order online: www.finishinglinepress.com
also available on amazon.com

Author inquiries and mail orders:
Finishing Line Press
PO Box 1626
Georgetown, Kentucky 40324
USA

Table of Contents

Apple Tree 1

Hunger 2

Bedtime With Aunt Leta 3

Blue Truck 4

Birth Story 6

Family Photo at Nine Weeks 8

Good Work for Small Hands 9

"I'm So Glad We Had This Time Together" 10

Peony 11

Gale Force Winds 12

Doormat 14

Crown for Annie 15

Early Insomnia 16

Sprout 17

Heart of Matter 18

I Am Lipstick 19

Mama Reads *Hawaii* 20

Spider 21

Are We Just Swallows? 22

Standing Long Jump 23

What's in a Shed? 24

To My Childhood Best Friend 25

Witch Movements 27

Names Never Mattered 28

Apple Tree

Twigs, leaves, grass,
a mass in the trunk's hollow knot—
an open bed to lay my hopes in.

I call upon sylvan friends
who hang in branches,
who feed on wind and rain.

I woo them with songs, place black walnuts
in this hole and cover them
with wood sorrel and violets when Mama is sick.

Three turns in dappled sunlight
to keep away ghosts who come
cold and wailing in the night.

Then I sit and wait, sifting
a fistful of dirt from one
careful hand to the other.

Hunger

In the backyard, I'm draped over the slide
under the mimosa, all frondy and pink
puff-blossoms shimmering like Easter candy.
Inside Aunt Leta and a roast, coffee in the pot
steaming. Uncle Bill in his undershirt
at the back table with the paper. Mom
smoking on the porch lost in gray thought,
40-something bones tired and torn between giving
up and her new motorcycle insurance man. I squint
at the blossoms blending sky into branches, leaves
into blossoms. The breezy tree sings me into flight.
I'm somewhere in the air, not hungry.

Bedtime With Aunt Leta

    We chant the Lord's Prayer,
line by line together

        as a streetlight streams yellow
          across her big bed.

    The scratch of sheets hard from starch
and Aunt Leta's thin polyester gown

        against my cold legs.
       Flat on her back, she smells of violets

and vinegar, her big belly humped
      under a sunbonnet quilt.

        I don't know my father.
        My kingdom is full of queens.

There's no such thing as trespassing here,
          our yards have no fences,

     just hollyhocks and lilies.
The alley connects us to Grandma's,

      Aunt Ginny's up the hill.
When we switch to Now

       I Lay Me Down to Sleep,
          I think, "If I should die before I wake,

I'll never see Mama again."
    She's out dancing

     with the man next door,
while I lie here

       listening to uneven snores,
          watching car lights shoot across the ceiling.

Blue Truck

Outside the Lutz Tavern,
a pickup so old
it must run on white
lightning. The navy blue cab
hulks above mythical
wheel wells. A skinny
twenty-something
in dungarees and a seed
cap, flicks a butt
to the curb, swings
the heavy door.
The rearview mirror
has slipped a bit,
side mirror cracked.
The engine rumbles
like a plaintive beast.
He spits through
the open window,
wrenches the wheel.
Big blue truck
just like the one
on that hot summer day
when Mama was so mad
she dumped her whole
cup of coffee
down the sink. The wiry,
whiskery man I saw
through the living room curtains,
leaning on a deep blue fender,
cigarette clutched between
thumb and forefinger:
My *real* dad.

His truck
right out front
where my step-dad Brad
usually parked
when he wasn't at work.
Big blue truck
just like this one,
thin man behind the wheel,
gears clanking as
he drives away.

Birth Story

The tectonic tremble of body
against body, like a sudden shake
and jar, scattering birds

into air, distorting
magnetic fields where personal
edges crack and slide,

fault lines forgotten—
potential magnitude unknown.
Like an aftershock, I am bones colliding

into bones, the third wave
from a late quake. Because who at 38
in '65 would want another?

With two just taking wing
and their father to the wind,
off the wagon after such a short time.

Short enough for cranes to call,
to let love take flight again.
Short enough to build a nest

and to make a seismic slip.
Let me be the afterclap,
the unexpected afterglow.

Not an afterthought but an accident plopped
into fallen feathers, broken twigs and dried
leaves in the crook of an old apple tree.

I'm an action in waiting,
complicit and silent and good,
watching as the Richter ratchets up.

I pick up on vibrations and gather
information to avoid the slow sideswipes.
I'm the afterimage of a collapsed nest,

the recalcitrant flicker on another branch,
preening my quivering plumes,
quickening a singular quill.

Family Photo at Nine Weeks

A magnet dimples her cheek. Mama's smile
draws you in. Hair coifed deep auburn,
curls pulled against opal. New light hides

the freckle-splash on her field of arms
jacked up to hold me. Her right
hand flat against my open chest,

filling it. My untested heart beats
just beneath. My own right hand
a coiled ball, brows bunched, already

deliberating at nine weeks in spring
pastels—blue for her, yellow for me—
and the tiniest, shiny Mary Janes.

Look closer. Electric currents cross
her forehead, blinds skew the view
from this Missouri clapboard porch.

Can you detect the late night scene
this family photo makes up for?
The demagnetized daddy fumbling

iron laces, boots tripping
over a slanted floor
to opposite poles in the dark.

My numerous infant needs.
Her long desire to be held
by something stronger

than herself.

Good Work for Small Hands

Knees in the grass, I pluck
    dandelions in April, scattered
        yellow buttons dotting the yard.

A small task to take
    my mind off, to get outside
        and use my body. What a familiar

sound, the quick pop
    of all that sunshine flooding
        my hands. At five, the act was

not distraction but love. On the ground
    for hours, idle, pondering
        the roly-polies under the elm.

Then a shift in breeze,
    waking the leaves
        overhead and a passing car

crackling gravel
    up the hill toward Belle
        Road. I'd look across

to the iris, large and off-
    limits, standing royal
        in their beards against

the garden wall, then I'd move out
    of the shade
        into the sunny grass

and carefully gather
    just enough brightness
        to place on the table for Mama.

"I'm So Glad We Had This Time Together"

Cicada-driven air streams evening.
Night-blooms of jasmine waft perfect

through the screen door to us there. Loud
leaf-laden drapery, burgundy and forest.

Still. Heavy against the ease. The TV set low,
flickering. Skinny butt next to four-year-old butt,

in the big square chair. After
play and her long day,

Melamine bowls on wide, nubby arms.
The Neapolitan pink, white, brown

dozes to soup in the tapering heat. As close
to love as ever. Tim Conway and Harvey

Corman banter like favorite uncles,
their words clip as they grimace-laugh.

Carol Burnett, long neck, eyes wide,
trips and scolds the men through pursed lips.

This slapstick holds the moment. Mama forgets
the day, and I'm not yet afraid

of the night. I lean forward,
Mama's hand on my back. She pats

a steady current just behind my heart.
I'm here. I'm here. I'm here. I'm here.

Carol Burnett sweeps the stage,
says, "So long," and tugs her ear.

Peony

They're crawling with ants—
everyone knows that.
Magenta May explosions
drooping like shredded mouths.

Most people don't know
I got mad one day. Broke off
my doll's leg, then buried it
in the front yard under the peonies,
where the ants could eat
her skin and drink her blood,
leaving nothing
but bones.

Gale Force Winds

I'm in a refrigerator box,
        inhaling the smooth smell
                of new cardboard, the heavy

duty delivery
        of household joy.
                Our single-wide trailer

not yet strapped
        to the ground. I'm
                in a box within a box,

landed here like Dorothy
        in a raw and odd reality:
                gold shag and my own

half bath. Beyond this box,
        Mom and Brad smoke, trouble
                about the rain rattle,

hard as rocks, the sway.
        This weather pounds.
                Our new metal roof roars.

Low hum below,
        a tone warning from the stereo.
                Emergency Broadcast System:

song sung blue,
        weeping like a willow.
                Then I'm scooped

out of the box,
        into the back seat.
               Wipers whoosh fast off beat.

The sky cracks
        with light. Mama flinches
                against the front seat.

In the basement
        at Annie and Carl's,
                safety.

We eat potato chips
        with French onion dip.
                Annie gives me a pad of paper

shaped like a goose,
        a Bic pen and a plastic glass
                filled with Royal Crown cola.

We are in Carl's workshop.
        Tools line the bench.
                Screws in old jelly jars.

An out-of-date calendar
        pictures a maid,
                her black uniform

printed on a plastic
        overlay that curls
                at one corner.

When nobody's looking,
        I lift the plastic,
                and I'm blown away.

Doormat

Thousands of little rubber
nubbins made to remove dirt
from the soles. Pointy and painful
under tender bare feet,
I cringe and hop, pretend
I'm a prisoner in a dungeon,
the Black Mat my punishment.
I get a naughty tingle somewhere
deep in my belly. Perhaps I am
to blame for all of this doom.
Or maybe I'm a sage,
practicing how to endure,
this mat my own bed of nails.

Crown for Annie

She aces the pile,
        slaps down two more,
                discards a useless deuce.
I feign the shock of a card shark,
        log the jack and king I know she holds,
                two spades looking for a familiar face.
Lament for the nine of clubs, lost
        between deck and hand and pile and hand,
                my own two nines held tight
like a pair of precious brothers.

        Everything I know about rummy,
                I learned from Annie.
The quick backward arch of the cards
        at the end of each shuffle. How to hold close,
                observe, wait. How even a small play
can add up to something good.
        I sharpened my math,
                discovered the pleasure of risk,
satisfaction of symmetry.

        Eating red velvet cake between rounds,
                we slid in sock feet
across the wide kitchen floor. We played
        until the black of midnight, cicadas singing
                through the dusty screens. She cut me no slack,
was in it to win. She shuffled, scoffed,
        whipped cards like deadly blades.

                Fifty-two years my senior, hair as white
as winter sky, teeth like shiny diamonds,
        this not-so-wicked step-grandmother
                lays down a run of hearts and wins again,
retaining the power of a beloved queen.

Early Insomnia

Every night, Mama falls asleep first.
I trace blue roses on the wall by our bed
with just a slip of yellow streetlight streaming
onto my swirling fingers. I lie awake waiting,

placing blue roses into vases in my head.
I listen for Mama's breath to lengthen,
conducting the air like a sound that lingers.
I try to breathe with her but she's lost in darkness.

My listening lengthens as Mama's breath
changes, and she rolls herself away.
Darkness surrounds us.
Her back to me, I lie awake wanting

the rolling night to change into day.
I'm alone in the dark and could wake her,
bring her back to me. But I just lie there
wondering why moonlight leaves me lonely.

Sprout
> *March 20, 1966*

Nine days old, leaves not yet on the tree.
She's alone on the sofa. Naked legs bloom

against dusty blue bouclé. In this picture,
everything's okay. It's all right.

But swaddle her—anything. Mimic her
lost cave. Wrap her tight like a bud,

seal her. Protect her unfurled shell.
It's the story of spring

sprung like shrapnel blast
in a field. The unexpected sprout

on the last branch, finally flowering
in all her writhing, pink-faced

perfume. Off camera, Mama
sobs in the tub. The reality of a baby's

sharp cries in the night, her constant
fist-waving dance captured

in an Instamatic flash,
cube twirling in the disheveled nest.

Papa gone. Somewhere
soothing a 20-year Navy wound.

Absence permeates the image, like a vacuum
cleaner roaring from the house next door.

But this blossom will make up the difference
for lost love. She'll just lie there

quiet as a violet—
and coo.

Heart of Matter

Amid marrow, new cells replace the old.
We are just bones transforming. At the base
of the aging apple, I kneel to face
bark gnarled like weathered skin, crevassed with gold.
I draw a body in the dirt—oval
stacked on four legs beneath, a tail. I trace
an outline among violets, such grace,
where I'm told they buried our dear sweet Rose.
Ten years my senior and half blind, her eyes
ever dripping sad, but I always saw
beyond them memories of where she roamed,
sun-dappled meadows for flying so high,
and somewhere, feeding wild wheat and raw
poppy, hidden long ago, her own lost bone.

I Am Lipstick

on a kerchief
embroidered with a lavender "B."
I am violets at the edges, white
cotton creased and tucked
inside. I'm a brown Bic lighter,
soft cigarette case, the quick click
to exhaled relief. I'm blue
ballpoint, a number
on a scrap, a checkbook-sized
pocket bulging with coins.
I am bills slipped neatly,
a broken swizzle stick
from Saturday night.
I'm a raffle stub,
dry clean ticket, grocery list,
Wrigley's wrapper,
a pair of gray leather gloves.
I am lozenges that muffle,
mints that conceal.
I'm the stale night air
seeped in between sets.
I'm lingering lines, the memory
of a hand, a glass. I'm a silver key
on a heart-shaped ring
in my mother's pocketbook,
hidden deep in the silky lining.

Mama Reads *Hawaii*

Bent arm, lit cig, long ash, crossed leg.
        Queen Lili'uokalani under pressure,
sugar sweet and up for grabs.

        Plumeria, pikake, pineapple pleasure,
pursed lips and a penchant
        for Michener. She's riding

the waves from her
        landlocked chair,
turning pages like seashells,

        raking sand on the shifting shore.
Lava builds its kitchen, her
        auburn hair turns black.

She doesn't hear the tiny peep,
        the squeaky query caught in air,
"I'm waiting" by the sea.

        She doesn't feel the ebb and flow
of little fingers at her feet, the prostrate weeper
        wondering when the chapter will be complete.

She doesn't see her longing
        daughter sprawled in shag, arms
outstretched like the shadow of a palm.

Spider

Near the hitch
on the front of the trailer,
underneath my bedroom
window—the hitch
where gangly Randy

from down the street,
must have crouched
to get a good look
between my parted curtains—
I saw a huge one,

fuzzy legs outstretched
as big as my palm.
Frantic at discovery,
it scrambled in the grass.
I shrieked, of course,

ran for Mama, who beat it
flat with a shoe, pounding
the ground with eyes wide
until it was gone—
except for one leg stuck to the sole.

Are We Just Swallows?

I go to bed to be alone,
to get away from the layers,
smoke cast like halos
around Mom and Brad.
The trailer so permeated,
my small bedroom window
stays open wide,
even in winter.
I hear them in the living room
on the other side
of my bookshelf, beyond
The Wind in the Willows,
Misty of Chincoteague.
They murmur after the news,
about money trickling down
like piss. Johnny Carson explains
horse-and-swallow theory, how
if you feed enough oats,
some will pass through to the road
for the swallows. Mom roars,
her nightly Carson crush.
Brad farts in his recliner.
The 25-years-of-service clock
chimes every 15 minutes.
My own heart beats,
a longing taking the shape of a drum,
skin stretched to its limit and holding.
Across the street, doors slam,
an echo of gunshots,
where a mad dad aimed
into his own home,
where mama and baby ached.
The trains down at the Purina plant
clank, then whistle long and loud
as they pull out
across Missouri fields,
heading west.

Standing Long Jump

I have the spring
but not the iron
for speedy locomotion.
Sprinting utterly
not an option.
I study grasshoppers,
ponderous in heat,
curious eyes
spinning in air,
back legs
bent on a blade,
yellow-green and strange.
I hunker
my haunches,
lift off
like a rocket,
soaring
into the unknown.
Four feet of chances
I don't want to miss.
I launch to impress,
feelers newly alert
to the fast boys
tracing the track,
sinewy strides
buzzing and flexing.
It's primal,
an exoskeletal urge
to jump, bound
into atmosphere—
anything but sit still
in the quiet
un‿‿‿‿y of long grass,
‿‿‿‿dibles grasping for
‿‿‿‿o devour.

What's in a Shed?

1. Wood. Two trailers down, my neighbor helps me build a table for my Barbies. I hammer together scraps that fall from his workbench.

2. Hammer. He shows my nine-year-old hands how to hold the heavy handle and swing with just enough force to drive a nail into wood.

3. Nails. Each size has its own bin for keeping things neat. When I drop one, the flat head and sharp point disappears into the gravel covering the floor.

4. Hands. His have dirty nails and are rough from long hours of work—even the palms are scratchy against my pale chest.

5. Rasp. His voice like a course file scraping a wooden object. When I say, "No," he backs away, hands sanding the air.

6. Yard stick. I am quick. I dash 100 home and rush inside. Lips press together firmly. Barbie doesn't need a table anyway.

To My Childhood Best Friend

Cleaning the skillet, I smell the sea
as eggs and iron crash against the stony sides

of my kitchen sink. Sometimes cool summer
mornings bring you to mind, a teeny bopper sunrise

tagging old clothes and chipped cups
for the annual sale. Or it's the steady afternoon

swell, when I'm flat hot and get a flash
of mulberry-stained feet in K-Mart sandals.

Pavement waves cresting into air. The wild
horizon cuts summer into slivers of glass,

broken floats in the dust. We walked some days
all the way past Skateland, cracked asphalt

pothole roads, kicking gravel ions along
Hwy 69. Trains cranked to a stop

across the sloped field down by the Purina plant,
where we never ventured,

never even let our minds drift—
rusted-out steel fork-lift clang beds

loaded with feed, brake sparks in the night.
Pet food production mysteries masked

by industrial metal trappings. Thick Missouri wind.
Except at night. I'd lie awake and wander there,

hear the tin and copper foghorn, explore the places
where I'm just empty, the ship-creak spaces

of my brain, places where you were filled up
with homemade fideo and crock-pot Rotelle dip,

places where your dad's cared-for cars
revved up top-down parade rides, and you slept

snug in the hull of your four-poster bed
like a treasure. How was it I was the one,

kissing boys and freezing your bra
in the night? You were quiet. I played it

cool. You fell asleep first. I stayed up
looking for the moon. You had all you ever

wanted in a backyard full of willow. I had an ache
for the sea long before I ever saw it.

You were a cliff under blue skies. I was a wave
crashing against you and pulling away.

Witch Movements

Out in the yard, I'm stacking bones
among purple blossoms, pert & perfumed. Violet leaves
help cast this spell. I'm slowly dancing on tender feet
beneath a skeletal tree. I'm by myself, but not alone—
spirited voices guide me twig to grass to stone.
In this life, five years I've known. I sleep
with bear & Raggedy Ann. But I see
from long ago, my lingering time as a crone,
foot to ankle, ankle to shin, knee to thigh to hip—
each bone atop another, stacked like stones. I move
through peonies, wilted pink and laughing, lowered
to the quiet brush of my palms, their dying petals dip,
falling to dark earth, and each falling another grove
where love and memory are forever stowed.

Names Never Mattered

Little purple flowers
    on Powell Butte, like tiny
fingernails on little fingers,
        these petal-dainty pinpoints
    dancing around a sun.
Along the path, their slim stems
    reach into dapple,
        feathery and fronded.

This profusion I need
    not name as I pass
into massive fir shade.
        Just as I never named
    the violets picked and bunched
by my small hands for Mama's
    ache nor the shadows
        of clouds as they passed
over our little house in South Park.

These flowers
    are wild and nameless,
more pale and profuse
        than the memories I hold.
    Like them, I am scattered
along this path, and they breathe
    their flower breath
        hot on my ankles as I climb.

Michelle Delaine Williams grew up in Missouri and now resides in Portland, Oregon. She was a 2018 Atheneum fellow at the Attic Institute of Arts and Letters, where she also co-hosted the Fridays on the Boulevard reading series for several years. Her work has appeared in *RAIN Magazine, Silk Road Review, VoiceCatcher* and *Verseweavers*. Michelle has a journalism degree from the University of Missouri–Columbia and works as a marketing writer for the tech industry. She lives with her husband and cat in the Pacific Northwest woods, where moss and mushrooms have replaced the hollyhocks and violets of her childhood.

www.ingramcontent.com/pod-product-compliance
Lightning Source LLC
Chambersburg PA
CBHW022127090426
42743CB00008B/1039